The Borders of the Sky

A Memoir

by
Mary Alice Cullinan

I would like to dedicate this memoir
to the little one inside
who is terrified of being seen
and yet wants to tell her story.

I would like to thank James Rahn and Vicki Ochocki
for helping me put this memoir into a readable document.
I would also like to thank my family and my dear friends
for their continued support throughout this process
and the various projects and journeys
I have embarked upon in my lifetime.

The Borders of the Sky

When I was 10 years old, I was hit by a car. I was walking home from a girl scout meeting with my friend, Vicky. It was a chilly Tuesday afternoon in early November. I carried an armload of books. We stopped at the corner until the busy two-lane road was clear and then we crossed. In the middle of the road, I remember turning to my right at the sound of a speeding car coming toward me over the rise in the road. I knew with frightening clarity I could not get out of its way.

The car hit me on my right side, tossing me up and over bushes in a front yard. I crashed into Vicky and she was thrown 17 feet. She broke her hip and sustained a head injury. My body landed in a heap and was hidden by shrubs. An ambulance came for her, but then a policeman found my shoe on the sidewalk and discovered me still unconscious.

They found my belongings and got another ambulance there. When my mother came to the door of our house about a block and a half down the street, she found a policeman standing there holding my penny loafer in his hand.

My ribs were broken along my right side. My right arm had a compound fracture. My femur was shattered, and they had to pick out slivers of bone and put a pin in from my hip to my knee. I had head injuries and was in and out of a coma the first couple of days. Trauma to my brain caused a lesion in my left temporal lobe which caused Grand Mal Seizures when I was in my teens.

I had to learn to walk again, and was constantly in pain. I asked my doctor when the pain would stop and he told me I'd have to learn to live with it. I didn't like his answer then and I don't like it now. I was small, with a quiet voice. I had always worked very hard to be heard in the few times I spoke up for myself. When I was told to get over my pain, once again I felt unimportant and easily dismissed.

Working very hard to do normal activities like playing ball and riding a bike, and also living with chronic pain, created the stimulus for my life's work of helping people on their path to healing. Whoever thought that a shy, introverted child with the kind of imagination that kept her spending much time on her own and in her own head, would work touching people for a living?

I am 68 years old now. I have done "bodywork" professionally for 30 years. That means I have assisted people relaxing, lessening pain, making changes to their body, mind and spirit through the medium of touch.

I am constantly amazed and wondrous at the incredible ability of the body to respond to my touch. It comes alive as my hands reflect an imbalance in the tissues to the body. Then I wait. Usually I feel a tendency of the person's system to move out of the pattern and change the area to one of more balance.

Many other areas of the body are affected at the same time, for there is a dynamic connection and intelligence throughout the body. When a change is made (which the body can tolerate because it is overseeing the change) all I have to do is follow and support this lovely process with my hands and my attention. Then there is a general easing of the tissues and a sweet shift in the ambient environment to one of peace.

Recently a young man came in who had been doing a lot of construction work. His shoulder was sore and not moving well. He basically had good muscle tone and his tissue wasn't injured from a tear as far as I could tell. The joint was out of balance. Moving it caused him discomfort.

I put gentle pressure on the back of his shoulder with one finger (at the subscapularis muscle) and one finger with pressure at the top of the shoulder (acromion process) and with my other hand applied gentle touch to the front (coracoid process). I held all three places and allowed them to balance themselves in relation to one another. I felt subtle shifting under my hands and allowed the joint to adjust itself. When he sat up, he felt it was comfortable and his arm moved well. We both smiled at how dynamic and simple the body can right itself with attention and support.

I am Diplomate Certified in Cranio Sacral Therapy, which helps the body to heal by removing restrictions in the nervous system. It was developed by John Upledger, a cranio osteopath. I also teach and practice Zero Balancing developed by Dr. Fritz Smith, which balances the body's energy with the body's structures - bones, soft tissue etc. Much of my work too, is Visceral Manipulation, which removes restrictions and tensions around the organs of the body. I have studied Myofascial Release and Massage Therapy and many other modalities. The first type of bodywork I learned was shiatsu.

When my kids were taking karate, one of the mothers at the dojo was a shiatsu practitioner. The instructor allowed her to work on his students from time to time. My kids loved it. I asked her to teach me. I suggested she'd charge me for a session and I could work on my kids while she showed me what to do. I had never received bodywork, but I saw how it made my kids happy.

I asked her to train me to do it for a living and she said, "Absolutely not! You can't make a living from it." I was a single mom with two kids, but I was determined. I was working, but began studying many different types of bodywork. In the process I began to get bodywork regularly and amazingly, the chronic pain which I'd had for twenty years went away.

I truly began to do be interested in bodywork. I had the smallest inkling it could help when I was eight and would rub my mother's shoulders. Her neck and upper back were like rocks and she'd say, "Mary, just grab my shoulders." I'd squeeze and roll my fingers and she'd talk to me and tell me how sad she was and how worried she was about everything. I'd listen and rub and she'd tell me she felt better even though I couldn't see much change. I believe she was seriously depressed then and very anxious, but at that time people didn't go for professional psychological help. So when she didn't withdraw into her room and close the shades, I was one resource for her.

I have seen thousands of people over the years and am encouraged by the persistence and ability of people to heal. I am awed by the many different ways people choose to live their lives and the various ways they treat their bodies. Even when people are trying to be careful, accidents happen, overuse occurs.

Poor sleeping causing tension, allergies, hormonal imbalances, and general stress to name a few, all can be reasons which bring people to bodywork to feel better. Each person, though, is a separate individual and their healing is unique to them.

I am always fascinated by people's stories. Diverse parts of people's lives are revealed in simple conversation. While piecing together the separate incidents, a frame of their journey takes shape. With different perspectives, a story could be portrayed in many ways - a hero's journey, a tale of persistence, a series of losses and wins, a love story, a career inspirational piece, a family saga, a spiritual journey. How it is perceived, takes shape in the telling. By chatting with someone, telling them one thing that happened and then another, the pieces come together gradually and the finished picture, like the creation of a sand painting, emerges in wonder.

Everyone has injuries. We survive day to day. And when we look back at that long stream of events that bring us into this moment, what are we hoping to have accomplished or received by now? Do we want to see our lives have sweeping, grand themes or do we want to savor the fleeting small moments that are precious and unscripted? Perhaps we want to do one kindness for ourselves and tell our story, project our small struggles out into the world for once, no matter who is listening.

I always ask my patients how they'd like to feel at the end of a session. "But I don't know what you are going to do?" they say.

And I say, "I orchestrate this, but you take in what you want and the changes you make are yours alone."

Recently I was sitting on the steps of a swimming pool. The handrail leading into the pool seemed to bend at the surface of the water. Staring at the railing calmly, it became more and more clear that this was the case. I asked myself, though, how it bent exactly as it met the water? I stood up and put my hand on the rail and followed its length as I walked into the pool. The rail never bent but followed a straight angle to the bottom. The light made it seem curved. To enter the pool supported, I needed to rely on what I could not see. I am haunted by the part of truth that relies on faith.

The head injury from the accident and 16 years of seizures have tampered with my perspective in many ways. I can remember the emotional landscape of an event and many small details. Some events I have lost completely, and I struggle at times to cover my lapses in memories for events and people. This struggle to remember is an ongoing part of my daily experience. Many things I have to re-learn as time has gone by, and often I have to sit and deeply focus; even then I may not recall things. This process, besides being maddening, also saps my confidence in being able to fully tell my story. I trust that the relevant parts will come forward with saving grace.

Teaching and doing bodywork has been very important in my life. I have also worked in restaurants for ten years as a waitress, a bartender and a cook. I drove and delivered packages for UPS for a year. I worked in an office as a technical recruiter for computer programmers.

I have studied meditation and yoga off and on since high school doing both much more intensely in the past 20 years. I have studied Pilates each week for 20 years, and tai chi for 21 years. In the last year, I have practiced the Tai Chi Sword Form. I studied martial arts for eight and a half years.

While work has occupied much of my time, my connection to Nature has been a compelling force. I love to walk outdoors and am grateful every day that I can walk. I have participated in many sweat lodges, and traveled to Utah Canyonlands, where I did a vision quest, meditating and fasting.

During my three days alone there, sitting quietly with my back to a cliff, thinking about my father who had died, a rather large, black bear came to me. He walked right up and looked closely at me. I was afraid (as I had been of my father), but asked him clearly to go away (something new.) He shook his head and scampered off.

I have hiked many beautiful places in Ireland. I've done ceremonies with a shaman in Peru at five sacred sites, including Machu Picchu. I have taken survival courses near the Pine Barrens in New Jersey. I have walked twice in the Susan Komen 60 mile Walk for the Cure.

A spinoff from my connection to Nature is poetry. It has always been close to my heart. From the time I was in high school, I have been touched by the words of poets. I love the change that happens when a picture that is being created with words takes a turn or leap and you land somewhere you least expected to.

You may have touched down with some surprise and perhaps with your heart a little more open.

I feel driven to find simple, precise ways to capture a feeling or an experience; to bring its essence sharply into the moment and shine a light on it. And I delight in seeing things in new ways, open to what arises with a new perspective. When I am moved by small, poignant moments in my day, I still try to find words to share these visions. My poems are written with a burning sense of urgency and then sit quietly on pages in a folder on a table beside my desk.

Another theme that has been important to me is a sense of home. Having it, losing it and then looking throughout my life to find it again. I have moved 25 times. My first home is the one place I am always drawn to when I am unmoored or overworked and lost. During those times, I dream about the "Farm".

Ninety acres, it was never a big working farm. It was the land I arrived at when I was born. When we moved to the city before I started school, it was the place I came back to in summers. When I was in college, I spent time there with my brother. When no one lived there, I returned and walked the land, visiting the trees I'd climbed and named, the woods and trails, the stream next to the house, the pond.

The land pulled me back like an umbilical cord that had never really been severed, but only stretched out. In the transition times of my life and in my dreams, it has tugged on my heart, entraining my energetic rhythms to the mothering heartbeat of that clay soil near French Creek. Its thumping song has told me I am home. It has soothed my spirit. I knew in my bones I was home and this was the one place I was safe and whole.

The farm was in Northwest Pennsylvania, 30 miles south of Lake Erie. My family had built the small house next to a creek, on fields cleared from dense surrounding woods. I can see clearly those open fields between long lines of trees, where, tired from exploring, I curled up under sunny skies and felt restored.

I was fascinated by the brilliant star-lit skies where, on summer nights, I would lie and wonder and dream and find my place in Nature - a place in the world around me.

My mother, who had inherited the land, loved flowers and insects. She had many flowers, and tied rows of sweet peas all along the back of the house. She had boxes and boxes of insects and butterflies and moths on pins, identified with their Latin names. She was an elementary teacher and eventually a librarian.

My father had taught at college and was a postmaster for a time - a city boy who, after serving in the war, tried to settle in the countryside, but eventually left the family at the farm and worked with various businesses, commuting from the city on weekends.

The farmhouse was practical and compact, with closets and drawers and shelves built into the walls. In the living room was a large window looking out across a large field with flowers and trees sloping down to the road, which led into the town of Cambridge Springs a mile away. In that front room was a carved wooden table with a tiffany type lamp and on either side was a rocking chair.

The wide, strong, wooden rocker was where my dad often sat. He was large with thick dark hair. To my ears, he had a deep resonant voice. Sometimes he lost his temper and it was terrifying. When he was in a big, gentle bear mood, he would rock us on his lap. I remember him singing "Old Man River" and rocking me. To this day, the memory comforts me and I feel I could rest indefinitely in that large safety net.

My mother's rocker was feminine like her. A gracefully carved, mahogany frame with spindle legs and curving arms, adorned with graceful flower shapes that were carved into the back. She sat there and sewed and sometimes read us stories. With patience, she encouraged us to learn and absorb what others had to teach us. One difference between my parents was: my mother would read us stories, my father would tell us stories. He encouraged us to discover what wasn't yet learned or taught.

Often we would sit together by the front window - my parents (Betty and Daniel) and my older sister, Toni, my older brother, Dan, and my younger brother, Ed. My nickname was Mac, but I might be called Mary or Mary Alice or Mac depending on the mood and circumstance (In moments of endearment, my mother called me her "little white rose" as I was very pale as a baby, with two little rose circles on my cheeks.)

We would watch great electrical storms that would come down from Lake Erie. I was scared and fascinated by the dramatic lightning strikes that danced on our lawn and the thunder booms that would shake the house. It was better than a movie. When a storm would come up, we'd have to pull laundry off the line and bring in anything outside that could be damaged.

Electricity came to us through a wire coming up from the road and one pole in the yard. Most of the electricity for our little house was controlled by a fuse box. As we were the only house for a distance, during a storm, if we were using a lot of electricity, it might attract lightning.

Our water came from a well in the yard and when the water was got to a certain low level, the pump would automatically go on and fill our tank. For that two minutes or so that the pump was on, making quite a racket, because we were generating a lot of electricity, we would feel very vulnerable to being struck by lightning.

So when a storm came, one of us would flush the toilet which would lower the water level in the tank enough to start the pump. If we had a full tank, and did turn on the water during a storm, we wouldn't set off the pump. (This procedure was so automatic that when we moved to the city, I continued to do it not even thinking why it was done. One time at a friend's house, my friend wanted to know why when the sky was darkening, I felt I needed to flush her toilet.)

We lived at the farm until we moved to the city, Pittsburgh, just before I started school. We kept the farm house to return to in the summers. But from the time I was born – 1949, in a hospital fifteen miles from the farm - it was a refuge whose paths and trees, and ponds and animals were a calming, nurturing place away from arguments, anger, hurtful words and actions that could erupt suddenly in my family.

We might be having a nice dinner, all of us laughing about some remembered event. Then suddenly, someone didn't agree with what happened or felt someone was challenging them and bitter words would come up. "You don't know what you're talking about. You don't know anything!" might be said in a nasty way. Or someone might storm from the table, throwing something or slamming a door.

I would be shaken when a pleasant time would turn into something mean. I would feel scared when anger exploded suddenly from nowhere. It would take me a while to calm down, and I'd tell myself not to get caught unawares again.

I remember the alcove on the way to the basement, where we kept fishing poles and baskets to collect berries, the radio around which we'd sit and listen to programs in the evening, the pound cakes my mother made for a church sale or a Grange social gathering. All these are placeholders of a family creating memories together - but the parts that keep coming back sharply and re-pricking my heart are the moments of angry mean words, too much drinking, storming out, banging doors, being slapped, hiding, crying, wishing I could disappear or live in the woods by myself.

I loved my family deeply and I fiercely wanted to feel completely accepted by each of them. I spent a lot of energy trying to prove to my siblings I was as important as they were. I hung on my father's words and would do anything for his attention, but this set me up to be put down as "Daddy's little girl."

I don't think I ever quite felt equal in my brothers' and sister's eyes, and spent a lot of time trying to prove I was funny or smart or at times sane enough to win a comfortable place within that group. They loved me, I know, but when they teased me and criticized me I took it very hard and felt left out.

I realize now, it wasn't so much my lacking that stopped me from feeling like I belonged, but the atmosphere of competition that was fostered at home, whether playing croquet or canasta or naming the presidents game. There was also an air of judgment and a general fear of any of us not living up to some incredibly high standards.

According to my father, we were all destined for greatness. We'd pull together in a crisis, but we never could maintain that sense of connection when things went back to normal.

I did put a lot of effort into trying to impress my dad especially. He would push us to achieve great things, and assured us we could do anything we put our minds to. He had big energy and grand dreams and I wanted more than anything to make him proud of me. I don't think I ever did. I think my having seizures seemed weak to him and a bit embarrassing. And when I broke with tradition in my youth and young adult life, he was bitterly disappointed in me.

When, after college, I didn't aspire to or thrive in a business pursuit, that was no more hope left for me. Once when we were in a corridor of a hospital visiting my mother, who just had a operation for breast cancer, he hesitated, shook his head and asked, "Are you still doing that stuff you do with the body?" My work, to him, didn't even have a name.

My mother, though she had wanted a happy marriage for me and a rewarding career, surprised me once. After her cancer surgery, with lymph nodes removed and her arm swollen to the size of a thigh, she let me, with gentle strokes, move the fluid by lymphatic drainage out of her arm and into her thoracic area, thereby reducing the pressure and pain. She looked at me, smiling sweetly, not quite understanding how this worked or what exactly I did, and said, "Mary, I'm so proud of you." That meant the world to me.

I loved my family very much, but fear was a presence in the environment of my daily life, lurking somewhere beneath the surface of simple family rituals. We were a Catholic family that followed the rules. We went to mass every Sunday and fasted before mass so we could go to communion. We went regularly to confession and made contrition for everything we could think of that we did wrong. It was difficult, but there was something satisfying about this unwavering structure. I even entertained the idea of becoming a nun for some time.

We lived and breathed the principles of discipline, sacrifice, doing the right thing, suffering in this life so as not to go to hell in the next. There were a lot of accepted addictions like smoking and drinking, and dysfunctions that go along with them. When I said or did the wrong thing, I was hit. It wasn't brutal or injurious, but it was physical. When I did something good, I was told not to dwell on it and to get on with what was next expected of me.

There were times of the family singing together while riding in the car, sitting in the backyard watching the sunset and playing croquet or catch, and building a kid's log cabin, but when I reminisce happy times, my mind quickly replays upsetting scenes: my father screaming and slamming out of the house, my mother breaking dishes and hiding in her room, fighting with my brothers and sister, and wanting to run away.

Perhaps inspired by my mother's reading to us, I loved to play that I was a knight. I fantasized about doing important and morally uplifting quests. I also liked to be an American Indian, living in Nature, a friend to animals. Values of goodness and helping also filtered through our learning at home.

When we left the farm and moved to the city, we lived in my uncle's house on Alice Street on the south side of Pittsburgh. My father was working as a stockbroker in town and my mother took a job as a teacher. It was a rundown brick house with a long sloping backyard full of brambles and undergrowth. There was a coal cellar and an alley, all good places to play and hide. I loved the feeling of being hidden, and the city did not offer all of the beautiful woodland areas of the country.

The sidewalk was cracked and broken because of the intense winters of freezing and thaw that eroded the pavement. But I learned to roller skate there, and even though there were no woods, I explored the alleyways and the winding networks of yards connecting many old homes.

School days I walked up and down the hills to St. Canice, the Catholic elementary school. The classes I attended were huge. We sat in alphabetical order and I had trouble because I was very self-conscious in front of others.

Feeling shy, I could hardly answer questions or speak when spoken to. My non-communication was thought to be insolence at times. I was a small very blond child, a tomboy who loved to play hard. I often laughed at the wrong times and dreamed of running away back to the farm.

My stockbroker father loved to play poker. He would gamble and we'd lose the house and have to move suddenly. We lived in five different houses in Pittsburgh. A couple of the houses were nice, but we could not truly settle in to any one of them for long.

When I was 16, I had my first seizure. I was an awkward teenager, who didn't like school. I would listen to music, dance and write poetry. One night when I had gone to bed late and was just falling asleep, I felt a deep shock. I cried out, fell out of bed, my eyes rolled up and back into my head. I rolled around on the floor in a fit, bit my tongue, wet myself, and sank into deep unconsciousness.

My mother was terrified and confused. She called an ambulance and I was taken to the hospital. She had no idea what had happened and it took me until days later to learn where I was and who I was.

My head injury as a child created a lesion in my left temporal lobe. At any time, pressure in that region of the brain could have overloaded the nervous system. As the nervous system is electrical, too much pressure would burn out the system. So the body's efficient way of discharging too much electricity is a seizure. It works to keep you alive, but is hard on the body in the process. The body is worn out afterwards, and that trauma has side effects like memory loss and disorientation and general discomfort.

My teenage years were like the perfect storm. I had added tension with hormones. Because I was very shy, I was not able to discharge the increased energy by expressing my feelings. I began to have Grand Mal seizures often.

Afterwards, I'd come to, disoriented and exhausted. My temples would feel like they were squeezed in a vise and my face felt like the skin had been stretched taut. My muscles ached as if someone had punched each one. My chest would be bright red. At these times, I would not even recognize my mother, who would be frantic. I also wrestled with the feeling of panic when I'd realize how little control I had and how a seizure could come on at any time.

After each seizure, there would be a period when I'd forget everything, even my name. I would do simple things, like color in a coloring book, and gradually my memory would come back. Things like math and history might have to be relearned. This happened a lot, and even with medication, the episodes were difficult to control.

My recovery time got better, the more it happened. I got used to drawing a blank with faces, but the medication (phenobarbital and Dilantin) dulled my feelings and my thinking and made me tired a lot. It also did serious damage to my teeth. Later, I learned how Dilantin affected my future and my family dramatically.

I missed a lot of school, but managed to finish high school with good marks. By that time, my parents were living apart. They never divorced (being good Catholics), but they could not get along. Besides, my father liked to have relationships with other women. Once he was missing for a year. We heard that the FBI was looking for him. I never found out the whole story, and then he resurfaced. He began to learn computer science and lived in Chicago and for a couple of years in Saudi Arabia.

I started college at University of Pittsburgh. I lived in the dorms on campus and then in dorms at a nearby convent. I struggled with my classes as I still had seizures from time to time and would forget material, fall asleep in classes, and get confused about assignments and classes. Somehow I managed to pass a number of the courses and continue.

I was still a young person who liked to go out on dates and began to feel quite an attraction for the opposite sex. I never went against the rules of religion and home and so I had never had any sexual experience, but I was curious. During this phase I had gone on a date with a young guy from Carnegie Tech, which was near the University of Pittsburgh.

One evening, after dinner, it was getting dark and we were walking through the park near campus. A man came out of the bushes carrying a gun. I was shocked and frozen. He ordered my date to lie down and pull his shirt over his head. He took his wallet.
He asked me if I was a student. I nodded. He took off my shoes and skirt and tights and raped me. I didn't know exactly what was happening as I was still naive. It hurt and I was wet. I thought it was blood on my legs, but it wasn't. He told me to stay in school, and then he told me not to get up or say anything and he left. I was aware but in shock.

I had to pull myself together and get dressed, then tell my date it was okay to get up. He was shaken too. We said very little. He walked me back to my dorm and then he went back to his.

The next morning, I got up and finally processed what happened. I went to the police station in town near school, but I couldn't go in. I felt ashamed and awkward. I was afraid to call home and upset my mother. I sat on a bench outside the station and from time to time, a policeman would come out and ask if I needed help. I kept shaking my head no and couldn't bring myself to talk. Finally it got late and I walked back to my dorm.

The next day, I felt angry and called a girl friend from high school who was going to Carnegie. I told her what had happened and said I wanted to go to the park and find the guy. She went with me and we searched for him. I saw no one suspicious, and besides, I couldn't remember what his face looked like. I was blank.

One day I walked over to the student union at Carnegie and when I entered the room, people looked at me and talked low. I realized then my date had told people at school. And he never got back in touch with me after that night.

I was hurt and felt betrayed by my date. I was angry at the man who, besides having physically violated me, took away my decision about whether to wait for marriage or to consent to have sex with someone I was close to. I felt rebellious, and rather than caving in and withdrawing, I acted out. I began to date a lot of guys after that. I was curious as to what I was missing, being so proper all my dating life.

I moved into an apartment with a group of people and eventually just dropped out of school. I stayed near the campus, worked a bit. I was engaged in having new experiences and trying anything and it made me feel courageous. But I also was filled with shame and self-loathing. I was in a self-destructive phase and often the thought of continuing to live felt like a heavy burden. If I slipped out of the life cycle by chance, I felt it would be a blessing.

I applied to and was accepted at Northwestern University. I went to stay with my dad in Chicago. At times, my father could be very generous and kind. He welcomed me into his little apartment with the Murphy bed that pulled out of the wall. He slept on the couch.

He seemed to think that when I came to live with him, he would be a great influence on my future. I don't think he realized how much I was struggling with day to day problems like memory and depression. "I have great plans for you, Mary," he told me when I arrived. "This will be a chance for you to get your life on track."

He was teaching computer science, which was new then. I spent a lot of time at the University's computer center, where the computer took up the whole room. He explained flow charts to me and I tried very hard to follow the complex logic patterns he was so enthralled with, but they didn't really grab me. I think he was disappointed in my lack of interest in this as a career. "Computers are the future," he assured me.

At times, my father could be scary and cruel. I remember one time he walked into the apartment in the evening. I had invited a young man to visit who was sitting on a chair in the living room playing the guitar. I don't know if he was upset that it was a guy there or that his space had been invaded, but my dad threw his briefcase down. He loomed over the guy, shouting at him. "You get the hell out of my place right now!" The guy fell over himself getting out the door.

My father then turned to me. He was now angry with me. He just stood there looking at me and shaking his head as if I was the most despicable creature he'd ever seen.

I had seen my father like this before and knew not to say a word but wait for him to come to his senses. I knew the pattern well.

My father would suddenly get angry and the transformation was startling and violent. It was like watching the Incredible Hulk emerge. His eyes would be wild, his color red, his voice booming and he'd look like he was going to explode out of his skin and do some damage. In an instant you would wonder how you ever felt safe with the gentle, mild-mannered, kind man who had stood before you a moment ago. This was the physically scary side of my father.

I never saw the young man again. I felt the fear for a long time and later apologized to my dad. I did not tell him then how unfair or embarrassed I felt. Within two months, I just quietly got my own apartment in his building and moved to my own space two floors up. I took a job on the south side of Chicago working in a printing firm. I began to take courses part time in anthropology, which I loved.

My father and I often played chess. Many evenings we sat and discussed various subjects for hours. We would talk about what was wrong with the world and how we could solve all of the problems that plagued society. It was a fun exercise in debating. During these times, talking with him myself and watching him talk to others, I learned intimately the psychologically scary side of my father. It entailed the verbal traps that would ensnare anyone who conversed with him.

Once again, there would be this sensitive, bright and interested guy who just wanted to hear what you thought about something. Lured in by his encouraging questions, you might share something you deeply thought or felt. Like a fish who doesn't know they are caught, you are given more and more line. You are careless about your explanation. Then he'd pounce, showing you the clear flaws in your logic and making you feel like a fool. People would avoid him after that, and I think he felt lonely quite a lot.

Sometimes he'd share some dream he had, and he'd get very passionate about it. I'd love to hear him describe how people could make a bunch of money or improve their lives if they'd make some creative changes. His eyes would shine with a brilliance fueled from far away, where his dream was brightly unfolding.

He'd paint a fantastic picture of the future. Most people would just tell him he was unrealistic or crazy and shake their heads. He'd alienate people in this way and I believe he felt very much alone most of the time. Later, he would tell me about it and seem so sad, and then I would feel sad. "Ah, Mary Mac, no one understands me." I really thought I was going to be the one person in his world to understand him. But in the end, I wasn't.

My father grew up in a socially sophisticated family and he could be charming as well as brilliant. People initially meeting him found him dashing and interesting. He had thick dark hair, strong cheekbones and bright, playful eyes. I believe my close friends who met him thought I was distorting my description of my father. I know that my fear and anger at him overshadowed my deep love for him.

Later, after I had been in therapy for a while, I wrote him a letter telling him how upset I was when he would put me down or intimidate me. He didn't answer so I called him. "Did you get my letter?" I asked bravely. "Yes, and I should come out there and turn you over my knee!" Once again I felt embarrassed and dismissed. I hadn't understood him and he hadn't understood me.

I stayed in Chicago near my dad for a little over a year, but then I got mononucleosis and was very sick and lost a lot of weight. I went back to my mom's apartment. "Oh, Mary, you're skin and bones." She let me stay, basically eating and sleeping until I found an apartment to share with others in Oakland near Pitt.

I took some classes and hung out at Pitt in the common centers, especially the Towers. I couldn't drive because of seizures, and it was hard to get around. I hitchhiked many places (it was more acceptable than it is today). Once I hitchhiked to Virginia Beach to see the sun rise for a summer solstice.

Once, with a friend, I hitched a ride at the airport to Mardi Gras. I accepted an invitation from a couple I met that day who had a private plane. They invited us to fly to New Orleans and back with them. Many times, I thumbed it to the farm. Once I hitched-hiked to Ann Arbor, to the University of Michigan for a 3-day Peace March with my younger brother; this was just before he signed up to be a marine.

At the Pitt Towers, I met a man who was divorced with two kids. He had been a postman. Paul was the proverbial hippie who had "dropped out." He was not tall, had long hair, a prominent nose, and piercingly beautiful blue eyes. He wore a bandana around his head. He loved to argue philosophy with anyone, play chess, and sit in on the bridge games I was often a part of.

He dropped acid often and loved it, but wouldn't touch other drugs or alcohol. He needed very little except cigarettes. He walked everywhere and would buy a Sporting News every day. That was the extent of his expenditures. He borrowed books from everyone and read them quickly. I had never met anyone as eccentric as Paul. I was intrigued and found him attractive and we started to go out.

I had very long hair then and loved the Peace Movement, living in jeans or long skirts and vests, sewing fabric and beads on them. We moved into a commune together in a very rundown section of Oakland called the Hill. About twenty people lived in this huge old house a friend of ours owned. People came and went, some students, some working, all generally people who didn't fit into conservative categories. It was multi-ethnic and interesting. We had a number of dogs there.

There was a single woman with a child who was a recluse. One guy meditated all the time. One girl from a rich family lived there until she joined a cult and disappeared. Her family came looking for her, but couldn't trace where she'd gone. There was great music blasting often from different rooms - The Doors, Led Zeppelin, The Allman Brothers, Crosby Stills and Nash.

I got a break on rent because I organized the food program, buying staples for the house and cooking from time to time.

Many people were taking drugs. I did experiment with drugs a few times. Some of the experience was good and some was terrible. I managed to get sick there, contracting hepatitis.

I couldn't really do much drugs as I was on medication already and it was a fine balance just managing that regimen. I was a proponent of natural foods and loved making foods from scratch with healthy ingredients. One day some of the people in the house asked me to make coffee in the house's big central kitchen. I think the group had just taken some kind of magic mushrooms which slowed you down and made you amazed at everything.

So I made coffee, and people sat around the table staring at their coffees, remarking at the wonderful smells or the cups and how their curved structures perfectly held this liquid which had no sustainable shape of its own.

I don't know if they actually drank it, and I complained to Paul later as we sat on the porch steps listening to the Pirates baseball game on the radio. "Don't worry about it, Mac, people are all crazy. If you try to figure out why people are what they are, you'll lose what little of your mind you have left." If this was someone else, I would have been offended. But it was Paul and so I just laughed.

I was taking birth control. I thought I was being radical as it wasn't sanctioned by the Catholic Church. Sex wasn't sanctioned either, but this was a time of Peace and Love so I took precautions. I took birth control pills.

I turned 20, living at the commune. I began to realize I was gaining weight and losing my waistline. I was naive again and thought I was just getting older. Paul and I hitch-hiked to the farm and spent some time in the run-down house no one was now living in. One day I felt something in my stomach move. I went to the doctor in town. He examined me and said I was pregnant. I asked him what I should do. He said to get dressed. He wouldn't say anything after that. I wasn't married, and to him it was very wrong.

We went back to the commune. I was scared but also very confused. I didn't learn until later that the Dilantin I took for seizures negated the contraceptive effects of the birth control pills. I never did gain a lot of weight and wasn't noticeably showing. I just looked chubby.

I took the bus out to my mom's one day and sat down with her. I told her I had a problem. She said, "Don't worry, Mary, I can handle it." I said, "I'm pregnant." She turned pale. "I can handle it. How pregnant are you?" I said, "Eight months." She burst into tears and began shaking. "I can't handle it!" she fairly yelled.

She called my father. He came in from Chicago and met me at a restaurant. He was furious at me. He said he had called a meeting with my grandparents, aunts and uncles to determine what would happen to my child.

I was flustered. "I have a right to decide what will happen to my child," I managed to say. My throat was squeezing itself so tight, I felt choked. "No!" he shot back. "You gave up your rights the minute you broke the rules and got pregnant!"

His face was dark as if a storm was brewing right in his brow. I was terrified. My future was getting sucked into a vacuum with the promise of that storm emerging. I stood up and made a dash for the door. Actually I waddled very quickly out the little restaurant and did not look back. I returned to the commune and lay low until the baby was born in the city hospital.

I read up on birth and practiced breathing, but I really didn't know anything and was terrified during labor that I was going to burst wide open. I wanted everything to be natural, but they did give me something for pain as I was frightened. The labor was eight hours long. I was able to nurse soon after, which was difficult for me at first, and I got a breast infection.

Eventually we found what worked and it became a lovely experience for us to share. I nursed my son until, at twelve months, he began to walk and lost interest in nursing. I was so afraid I wouldn't know something crucial about taking care of an infant - something everyone else knew - so I read many books. The books did nothing to reassure me. However, I had never felt such a deep, transcendent connection to an individual as I did as a mother to this beautiful, pure, miracle baby. I suddenly felt, this is the reason to live. And I felt it strongly and clearly for the first time in my life.

Shortly after my son Todd was born, I took the bus out to my mom's place. I held him out to her and she shook her head. "Oh, Mary, I just can't."

"Please, mom, hold him for just a minute. I have to go to the bathroom," I told her and lifted him towards her again. She stood firm, her arms crossed in front of her, her eyes filled with tears. "I just can't. I just can't. You don't understand. This is all wrong."

She couldn't bring herself to embrace him. "You must understand how this goes against everything I believe." My having a child out of wedlock to her meant our souls were lost and she was in no way allowed to condone this transgression and be sympathetic.

It took some time, six months, and then my mom softened and asked to hold the baby. In the end, she could not resist what a lovely child he was and came to love him dearly. My mother was easily hurt, slow to forgive, but she had a kind, sweet, child-like heart herself.

Paul and I did little things to make money. We made and sold macramé, and raised German shepherd American Kennel Club certified pups and then Siberian Huskies. We lived in the commune and then in an apartment in an old house. When my son, Todd, was almost two, we split up. We had become more like brother and sister, and we had basically stayed together as long as we did for our son.

Paul and I both were sad about the split. He wanted Todd to stay with him, and we argued about it. Eventually we agreed Todd needed to be with me, and we needed to move on and meet new people while we were still young.

Paul moved out, and I moved into another commune. I began to explore communes that were rural, and visited and stayed at a couple in the south. During this time, I got back in touch with Mack, a guy I had dated in high school and at the beginning of college.

I had met Mack at a CYO dance (Catholic Youth Organization). He went to Kent State and I to Pitt. We had dated then, but we eventually drifted apart. He had moved from Pittsburgh to Philadelphia. Looking for communes, as I was traveling by train and passing through Philly, I asked him if he'd like me to stop by and visit him.

He encouraged me to come, but he was shocked when he met our train and I had a 2 1/2 year old child in tow. We had a nice visit and made a good connection. I wound up getting my things and making my home with Mack and his dog Harvey, in the Homesburg section of Philadelphia.

After a year, we moved to a rural suburb of Philadelphia - Schwenksville - and rented a cabin on the grounds of an old summer camp - 50 acres on the Perkiomen Creek. The cabin was very rustic, and I felt thrilled to be back in the "country" again.

Shortly before we moved, I found I was pregnant again. This time I recognized my condition right away, even though I was unaware of the dilantin/conception connection. I adjusted to taking care of a house, having a garden and spending more of my day living closer to nature. I began baking my own bread, grinding the flour, making my cereal and my own yogurt.

My daughter Janel was born in February, a very cold time which was a bit of a challenge in the rustic cabin. She was open and loving from her first moments. Mack went to work all the way to The Navy Yard in South Philly every day of the week.

I wasn't driving, but was pretty content with the kids and dogs and the land and stream. We'd walk and explore, grow some herbs and veggies. For the Bicentennial - 1976 - we had a three - day party and invited friends to come out and camp on the land, play folk music and cook out. It was fun and for that time, things seemed simple.

We eventually moved to Spring Mount, not far from there and rented a regular house. I was 27 and after wrestling with memory problems, impaired functioning, and being very tired and flat in my feeling, I knew I had to get some help. Also I had not been able to control my seizures, which would occur from time to time at night if I got too tired or was upset emotionally during the day.

I began to see Dr. Courtney Baker, who was a psychiatrist and an orgonomist. He felt with time I might be able to get off my medication, but I would have to learn to comfortably feel my emotions and express them. I was not graceful with the process and was easily frustrated.

This became a difficult time between Mack and I, and we began to drift apart. We had fallen into a pattern of how we related to one another, and a change in how we did this was like climbing a mountain on your knees. It didn't feel right to either of us.

I had a hard time standing up for myself, and I could feel that my emotions weren't comfortable for him. I retreated, and felt walls going up between us.

At one point, Mack had an opportunity to advance in his work, which would entail a transfer to central Pennsylvania, a couple of hours away. I encouraged him to take it.

When he accepted the position, I found myself sitting beside him on the porch after our kids had gone to bed. "I think this will be a good thing for you," I said. "Yes," he agreed, "a new start. And there will be a lot of countryside there. You'll like that."

I tried to picture us all making a home together. There was a lot of caring and a good bit of history between us. But then I thought about me trying to follow the directions of therapy and express my feelings. I could see myself once again, rather alone with my emotions and my pattern of feeling frustrated and shutting down.
This just set me up to have an episode and sabotage the work I was doing. I wanted so much to be free of seizures. If I was going to be healthy, I'd have to make a choice that didn't feel wretched. It would break up the family and yet, if I didn't, I felt I'd lose myself.

I found myself saying, "I don't think I can go with you."

"What? What are you talking about? I thought you wanted this."

My throat was very tight. It hurt and was hard to breathe, but I was trying to be true and open here. "I just can't come now, I need to get myself together. When I do, I'll come out." I never did.

Mack was very connected to both children, Todd and Janel, and he was not happy about breaking up the family, but he was willing to trust that in the long run, separating during this time was for the best. He moved, and we visited each other often and had good times with the kids. The more we were apart, though, the more we saw it was healthier. Eventually Mack met his future wife, Kathy, at work. And I continued to work very hard in therapy.

Dr. Baker treated me with a mind/body therapy called Orgonomy. Orgonomy, developed by Wilhelm Reich, focuses on reestablishing a healthy flow of life energy called orgone energy. The premise is that when we are healthy in body and mind, we are open, feel good and have vital energy.

When we are not functioning in a healthy way because of negative experiences of the past, we become contracted. This is reflected in our personality and the patterns of tension we hold in our body.

This body armor, as it is called, and our patterns of how we interact may be attempts to protect our wounded self. By learning how open these layers of armor in a safe way and begin to operate in a more authentic way with ourselves and others, we begin to experience our lives in a more natural, creative, expansive way.

The work I did with Dr. Baker was very difficult for me. Holding in my feelings caused my eye area to be tight and unmoving. This type of eye restriction blocks the release of energy, which can then build up in the body, necessitating a seizure in its dramatic release of tension.

I had to learn to recognize my feelings and then express them, freeing up my eyes in the process. This wasn't a smooth process and at first, it was hit or miss. When a seizure was coming on, I'd get an aura. This was a strange sound that I'd hear, and I'd get an odd feeling in my body. If I could respond to this sensation, not panicking, but moving my eyes, not letting them lock and trying to release any emotional buildup, I might stop the seizure.

Many times, I'd try, but couldn't quite do it and I'd watch myself losing my balance and my consciousness.. This was one of the most difficult things I have ever done. My first instinct when I felt a strong emotion was to just make it go away.

The last thing I wanted to do was tell someone how I felt, especially if they were upsetting me. After a day of keeping things held tightly, I'd be tired and just want to sleep, but often my body was full of unexpressed energy.

I recall feeling an aura - that funny buzzing in my head - as I was about to fall asleep once. I panicked and tried to jump up and stop the seizure, but I lost my balance, fell over backwards and hit my head on the night table. The walls of the room spun away from me and I was devastated as I sunk down into darkness, as if I were slipping underwater.

I started to work with the doctor to get off my medication and that process took three years - decreasing the dose, feeling overwhelmed, having a seizure and starting all over again at a full dose. At 32, sixteen years after my first episode, I had my last seizure.

Dr. Courtney Baker was a tall man with red hair, a fair complexion and boyish good looks. In our sessions, Dr. Baker calmly said whatever he perceived and did not sugarcoat anything. He did not let me skim over my feelings or reactions, but pushed me to be honest and straightforward in my interactions.

I felt like he was ruthless and often I felt angry at him. This was fine with him as we'd look a little deeper and see where in past experience the roots lay hidden. They were often entangled in the anger and hurt I felt especially towards my father, but also towards some teachers and past friends.

He helped me feel it was okay to have strong feelings, that I wasn't a bad person because I felt anger or hate. I was just a person with soft parts inside negotiating a world that could be painful at times. And if I didn't accept and process the bad feelings, I couldn't get to the good feelings and enjoy them.

He might press on my jaw or lower back, deep in the fascia, where strong emotions get stored. Sometimes he'd have me trace the edges of the ceiling, following its contours with my eyes. This movement also brought many uncomfortable feelings to the surface. One minute I'd be feeling blank, and the next moment there was this dark tunnel of rage or maybe fear that would surface with the pressure or movement.

A memory might come up. Whereas before I'd recall the details of an incident, now the emotional component would be clear and present. And there'd be the sickening feeling that accompanies a strong feeling. I would desperately want to run away from it. But Dr. Baker would make me confront it.

I'd yell or cry, saying what I felt. At first it was hard for me to just say, "Stop it!" and mean it. He had me experience the feeling, express it, and finish up with it for now. My body would greatly relax and I'd feel a softness of life energy move through my tissues.

I remember being in Dr. Baker's office after a particularly intense session. I felt I was doing well and gaining ground. He was helping me get off medication, and he was helping me get on with my life. I was feeling very hopeful and I asked him point blank, "So, do you ever feel I will be completely healthy?" Dr. Baker lifted his eyebrows and hesitated. I pushed him. "Really. Do you think with all these changes I'm making, I'll be normal?"

He looked clearly into my eyes, smiled and then shook his head. "Not really."

I felt my cheeks color and a heat rise in my throat. I wanted to explode. I wanted to scream, "No!" I wanted to curl up in a ball and disappear. How could he say after all this time I still wouldn't get a shot at being fully functional? "Why?" I asked.

He spoke slowly and carefully, but told the truth. "Too much damage."

After that I felt I wanted to show him I could be completely healed. Over the years I came to realize that certain unhealthy reactions were still in my core. From time to time, I see my tendency to hide. Also I get hurt very easily and I can get angry just as quickly. These parts of me are still there. I can work with them now and I can find balance and peace within, with awareness and patience.

I still have auras from time to time, but I have so far been able to control them with focus and eye contact. My worst fear is that it will happen again and I will lose a lot of ground again. I have to remind myself that we all have fears we learn to live with.

After Mack and I split up, I was much more on my own in the world - driving, working in a restaurant, taking care of kids and continuing in therapy. I didn't have time to be discouraged and stuck. I worked hard and made friends with some of the other waitresses - friends I have to this day. I moved to Collegeville and the kids and I lived above an antique clock shop.

I was determined to get a better job, so while my kids were in school during the day and I wasn't at work, I took courses at Ursinus College. I got my bachelor's degree in English. I hoped to eventually work in journalism.

In order to go to graduate school at Temple University, I applied for a work/study program there. I was accepted, but the work program didn't pay enough for me to live and raise two kids. So I continued with restaurants, cooking in three of them, bartending in three of them and waitressing in the others.

I never wanted to feel as helpless physically as I had when I was attacked in college. My deep wish also was that my children would never feel helpless either. My children were taking lessons in martial arts and I felt inspired by their progress. So during this time, I began studying martial arts, taking classes one night a week.

I studied karate for seven and a half years, competing in tournaments and winning some trophies. I also studied aikido for a year, which I loved because it taught me so much about moving with energy and incorporating a bit more grace into my movements than I was used to.

During my last bartending job, a salesperson from a firm in Bala Cynwyd encouraged me to apply to be a technical recruiter for data processing at his firm. There I could get medical benefits and make more money. I applied for the job, and there I met David. He was one of the people who interviewed me and he was the one who trained me.

On my first day of work, David told everyone at the morning meeting what his wife had told him the evening before. She had met someone and was leaving their 10 year marriage. They had a 2 ½ year old daughter, Karen. I was shocked. I didn't know what to say. "Congratulations!" I said heartily. He looked at me quizzically and then laughed. I think this broke the ice between us and paved the way for us becoming good friends.

His perseverance at teaching me the fine points of interviewing, writing a resume and keeping in touch with candidates helped me become a good recruiter.

I hated being in an office and it was a difficult adjustment. I learned what it is like to work in an office setting, with deadlines and quotas and inter-office politics. David and I would often go to lunch together. We would talk about work and our kids and the news of the day.

Often he had to calm me down if someone was fired, or the boss was ranting about clients or our work. I was very sensitive to the ups and downs of office politics. Our casual lunches turned into going out for dinner or a movie or an evening shooting pool. We were both a bit afraid of being close to someone again, so we took it very slowly. We had begun a relationship, but didn't tell anyone at work.

In 1989, after three years of dating, we decided to move in together, blending our families and finding a house to rent in Plymouth Township. During this time I had begun to study shiatsu - first from my friend, then from an institute. I studied Massage Therapy and got certified.

By the time we moved in together and I gave notice at work, I was able to begin a bodywork practice on my own. I worked in my home and in several chiropractors' offices during different days of the week. I continued to study, taking nursing courses in Anatomy and Physiology at Montgomery County Community College.

When I took Cranio Sacral Therapy training, I knew I was doing what I was supposed to be doing. I was working with the nervous system, and began to understand a lot of my neurological restrictions. I was able to help people with conditions such as migraines and stress and insomnia, even reducing the incidence of seizures in some cases.

One time I even worked on a 10 year old boy who had been hit by a car as I had been at that same age. He had broken an arm and leg also. He had a head injury which caused processing and memory problems. Working with him stirred up for me memories of being vulnerable and hurt.

It was strange for me to be working from the perspective of a helper rather than the injured one. We were able to get things balanced again. We had a nice relationship in the process because he discovered someone could experience the process that he was struggling with and come out the other side.

Both of my parents died in 1991. My father, who lived in Chicago, fell on ice and broke his arm; he died of pneumonia in the hospital. It was sudden, but I believe he wished this to be his exit as I think he suspected he was developing cancer from years of smoking.

My mother died three months later in Florida when her breast cancer came back full force. Her medical team was amazed at how long she lived considering how weak her body had become. I think her spirit carried her the last few miles. 1991 was the worst year of my life.

In 1992, when my daughter was 16, I took a train trip with her around the U.S. My son Todd wasn't interested, and stayed with friends. My daughter and I traveled to Chicago and during the eight hour transition, we visited the city.

We took a southern route and got off at Santa Fe. We rented a car and explored that town and Taos. We got back on the train and got off at Flagstaff Arizona. We rented a car and explored Sedona.

One day we hiked to the bottom of the Grand Canyon. It was amazing. We stayed overnight and the next morning walked back up. I had encouraged my daughter on the way down; she encouraged me and gave me strength to get back to the top. Just as we got there, a huge storm broke and we made a dash for the car just in time.

We got back on the train and travelled to Los Angeles. We rented a car and drove up the West Coast, visiting many beautiful towns like Santa Barbara and San Luis Obispo. We stopped at Esalen Institute, where I took a course in Zero Balancing. It was a lovely, meditative space. I studied during the day and my daughter participated, helping out in the kids' programs.

I met Dr. Fritz Smith, who had developed Zero Balancing, a cutting-edge bodywork that would integrate the Cranio Sacral Work and balance someone out energetically. I saw this work would support all the work I was doing. I loved the work and the people teaching it, and set out to getting certified and becoming a teacher for ZB, as it is called.

After class, we continued to drive up the coast of California, visiting small towns along the way and checking out all the beaches. We drove to Northern California and camped in the Redwood Forest with the little tent we had carried with us.

That night, our tiny tent pitched in the middle of nowhere under a great redwood tree, we huddled together. We heard an animal foraging around outside, bumping into the outside walls.

We stayed very still, holding our breath until it was quiet again. "Do you need to go to the bathroom?" I asked her finally.

"Yes," she said, "but I'm not going now!" We laughed and waited until daylight to venture out. The beautiful forest felt safe again.

We stayed a few days in San Francisco, and loved the culture and food and the casual atmosphere as we walked through the city and explored all the neighborhoods.

We took a train then that wound around the northern U.S. It had an observation car. We learned a lot about the west and its history, as people spoke about the places we were seeing. We walked around Denver during a five-hour layover. In Chicago, we caught our train back to Philadelphia, returning with new knowledge and a sense of the expansiveness, beauty and diversity of the country we live in.

During the time we lived together, blending our families, David and I often talked about getting married. I was always so afraid to marry as I never wanted to get a divorce, and my parents seemed so unhappy and stuck in a bad marriage. We were in love and committed to one another, but it was hard to take that final step into matrimony.

One day, we had just watched a movie, *The Wedding Singer*. It was a sweet story about a guy who as a wedding singer was always close to people marrying. Because he had been hurt before, he was always afraid of marriage, until he fell deeply in love with someone he had become friends with and was working for.

The story touched us both. My eyes were teary and David said to me, "Why don't we just get married?" We didn't need to get married for the kids or for insurance or any reason I could think of. Not one to get caught up in practicality I said, "Why not?"

So in 1999, when I was 49, I married David at the big farmhouse that we rented. Built in the late 1700s, it was on 50 acres and was the grounds of a children's summer camp. We were married outside in our large yard on a lovely summer's day - June 13th. The weather stayed beautiful at our house.

My son gave me away. My daughter was my Maid of Honor and my step-daughter, Karen, was my bridesmaid. We had a huge white tent in the yard. We exchanged vows that were a combination of Catholic vows and Jewish traditions (breaking the glass), Celtic prayers and American Indian blessings.

About 70 of our friends and family came to celebrate with us. It was cloudy at the beginning of the ceremony, and just as "I now pronounce you man and wife" was said, the sun burst through and radiated light over us all. Everyone cheered.

We had a simple buffet and many flowers everywhere. David compiled CD's with our favorite music, which poured out through speakers on the porch and carried across the grounds. My one wish for the wedding was to have everyone dance. And we all did! Later in the evening, when David and I were straightening up the yard, we learned it had rained all around the area, even raining out the Phillies game!

We honeymooned in Paris and it was delightful. We wandered around all the little streets, took the metro to Montmartre and Père-Lachaise Cemetery (where Jim Morrison and Oscar Wilde are buried), wandered through many museums like the Louvre and Rodin and Musée d'Orsay with its lovely impressionist paintings. We tried all of the French food delicacies such as escargot and almond croissants.

We stumbled upon an insubstantial restaurant that was tucked away on a side street. It was called "L'Apostrophe" and we immediately felt as if we had discovered our very own little "shangri la". The dark space with perhaps four tables in the front room, and mismatched comfortable chairs, enchanted us.

The husband and wife who ran the place were sweet and took special care of us. We loved the salad/antipasto bar and the special little wine cocktail they made for us. L'Apostrophe provided an atmosphere of intimacy and intrigue and called us back to it.

I had studied French since high school, been a French family's mother's helper as a teen, studied it in college, and belonged to a group speaking French for years. I looked forward to being able to communicate in French instead of being an American who relied on everyone else speaking their language.

David had had some French, and we were getting a kick out of asking shop keepers about an item or the museum people the price of entry etc., the metro people about a stop. We'd congratulate ourselves at negotiating this beautiful, foreign city. All of the meals were a bit different than what we were used to and our experience with them turned into some surprises but usually delights.

One evening, in an upscale restaurant on the left bank, we prepared to order our dinner. The atmosphere of the dining room was tasteful, with dark wooden walls, large mirrors, candles in wrought iron holders, the tables covered with crisp white tablecloths.

The waiter had striking chiseled features and was dramatic in his bearing (if not warm and welcoming), moving like a dancer and holding his shoulders high as if he owned the place. After we successfully ordered a kir, white wine and cassis (which was becoming our pre-dinner ritual), he came to take our order.

I held the enormous menu and recognizing the word "agneau" (lamb) in the title, I tried for my best French accent and asked for "Cerveau d'agneau dans du bouillon."

The waiter looked down at me disdainfully, "Madame, you have just ordered the brains of a lamb!" He shrugged his shoulders and continued, "You want the chop."

I was humiliated. My Irish was also up. I wanted to shout at him, "Yes, you insolent creature, that is exactly what I wanted! Perhaps you could use some brains yourself!" But I didn't. I nodded, chastised. When he left, David and I smiled at one another. This was an awkward moment, but later we laughed about it. We would tell the story of the arrogant French waiter and the naive American in Paris.

Another year, David and I traveled to Ireland. He explored a lot of the island with me for a week, and then returned home. I continued on my own to explore the walking paths and small towns. Ireland was lovable, and it reminded me of the rural areas of my childhood on the farm.

My father's family had come from western Ireland, County Claire around the town of Cooraclare and the townland of Danganella. I had a hard time finding exact dates to confirm our connection to the many Cullinans in the area, but everyone I met assured me we were related. I felt a strong connection to the land and returned five times to visit, take classes in Gaelic, study Yeats and visit friends I had made.

One time, the town of Kiltimagh offered me an "artist-in-residence" opportunity. I stayed in the refurbished train station for three weeks for free, and was able to write and participate in what was going on in the little town. I taught some bodywork classes and was surprised at how much the people enjoyed learning how to do simple bodywork techniques on family and friends.

That encouraged me, and on another trip, I came back and set up two classes each in six towns, and taught gentle touch techniques to the locals. I had them fill out questionnaires to see if they liked it, and if they thought it was valuable and something they'd use on family or friends. Everyone was very positive, and I was encouraged. Who said the Irish wouldn't go for touch?

I tried to get a grant to do it on a larger scale. I thought it would help bring people in healthy ways, but that it might be something difficult to pay for. I tried very hard to get it funded but failed. But it was a lovely experience, and I learned that the language of touch was a wonderful bridge between cultures and generations and sexes. (Kids, older people, men and women all were willing participants in these classes.) I created a non-profit company - Meri-Mac, Inc. - to teach healing techniques to family and friends, complete with a video and manuals; getting funded has been difficult.

My husband and I have learned Italian and traveled a lot to Italy- the Italian Riviera, Tuscany, the Amalfi Coast and Sardinia. We also love to visit England. Niagara Falls was one of our favorite vacations, walking all around the Canadian side of the falls.

Nova Scotia was a place we visited on a cruise and enjoyed, walking through the towns at each stop, and especially Quebec. We've traveled a couple of times to the jazz festival in Montreal, which is also a lovely place to investigate on foot, especially Mont Royal.

When I turned 60, my husband threw a birthday party for me. This was the first actual birthday party I had with invited friends, that wasn't the family after dinner having a cake with candles for me. Nice, but I have never quite gotten over being shy, and so enjoyed being in the limelight more in retrospect.

A few years after my work with Dr. Baker was complete, I still wanted to continue to heal my life, but I wanted a change. I began to see another orgonomist, Dr. Louisa Lance. She was a petite, pretty woman who was always dressed very smartly and had a gravelly, low voice. She had been the head of the women's unit for a major mental health facility in the suburbs of Philadelphia.

I wanted to find a peace within myself about the past, and not let the automatic responses to a situation be triggered by past associations. I also wanted to continue to learn how to identify my feelings as they came up and be able to express them when I chose.

Dr. Lance could be very compassionate if I was truly hurting. She'd verify that what I was feeling was totally justified and I should not judge my feelings. "You feel how you feel," she'd say. "You can't control that. It's not right or wrong, it just is. You feel what you feel and then from there, you decide how you want to deal with it."

I admired how she was able to be painfully honest with me when we were working, yet she never looked down on me. I might be complaining about how someone treated me and I might get so focused on how unfair someone was to me and she'd say, "Mary, get over this. Right now you're just feeling sorry for yourself."

She encouraged me to stand up for myself and not worry about what everyone else was thinking. She taught me to honor my feelings and to be respectful of myself. Over time, I became very close to her. She was an authentic, tough, caring woman. As I put more time into my work and was feeling more confident and clear, I stopped seeing her professionally, but kept in touch with her.

She developed back problems that couldn't be treated. She was in a lot of pain. Where she had smoked cigarettes and drunk coffee often, now she did so constantly. She had contracted gallbladder cancer, and deteriorated quickly. I saw her one time and she looked like a ghost. She wasn't eating and couldn't drink. She barely managed to hold some ice chips in her mouth. I stayed beside her for a while, just talking and then thanking her for her help. I wasn't even sure if she understood before I said goodbye and took my leave.

Over the next two weeks, I checked the obituaries, but found nothing in her name. On an impulse, one day I stopped by her house. The gardener let me in. Dr. Lance opened her eyes, looked very animated, and asked the nurse to step out. "Mary," she said enthusiastically, "how are you? And Todd and Janel?"

Her clarity and projected energy was like a miracle. She seemed ready to joke around or take on some problem if I needed that.

When she picked up on my amazement, she said, "You gave up on me didn't you, Mary? I'm surprised, you never give up!" We laughed and talked. Shortly after that, I left. Later that night, she died. Once more she showed me how a person could show up a hundred percent even at the edge of life.

When I was 19, I was treated for Hepatitis B in a clinic in Oakland for five months. In my fifties, pain in my right side and a blood test revealed I had Hepatitis C. I took many supplements and Chinese herbs, got regular acupuncture, and had two liver biopsies. When I was 66, a drug was developed that was shown to cure Hep C. My gastroenterologist was supportive when I suggested it and he followed me as I took the two month course of medication.

At the end of that time, blood tests showed the virus was gone from my system. I'd like to say I felt totally relieved, but once you have thought of yourself in a particular category (such as "epileptic"), it's hard to believe you can ever allow yourself to sink into a carefree state again. (This kind of vigilance leads me to believe I have some PTSD from the various traumas over the years.)

I have loved teaching bodywork, especially Zero Balancing. It has been a nice balance with seeing people for individual sessions. I wrote a book called *In Session*, which is a fictionalized account of a Cranio Sacral, Zero Balancing therapist and a woman whom she is treating. It describes eight sessions, and you see the work from both persons' perspectives.

When my granddaughter, Juliet, was four, she moved with my son and his wife to Colorado. She had stayed with us often on weekends since her birth. I missed her terribly.

Living in an apartment, we couldn't have dogs, which I had loved and grown up with. So I rescued a kitten, Animé (French for animated) and I learned a lot about how to love a little creature who was wired to be independent. She likes to be with me at times, but when she wants to be left alone, she is clear in drawing her boundaries. She is painfully honest. She is a pleasure to be around - aware but serene. However, when I am petting her too much, she will put a paw on me, nails out. She is still purring all the while.

In 2014, we bought a townhouse in Blue Bell, PA. This is the first house I have ever owned, and I am finally beginning to feel like I am home. I still dream of the farm, but it is now a sweet memory from childhood. The image of the farm comforts me, but doesn't tug on me to return in order for me to be complete again.

I fell and broke my wrist in four places a year ago. I had a plate and nine screws put in. Once again, as when I was ten, I had to be patched together. I have crumbly bones like my mother (osteoporosis).

Rehabilitation was a wonderful way to learn in a new way about how I can still recover. I exercised the hand and strengthened the compromised muscles and ligaments every day. I was back at work in three months.

I have studied Mindfulness and Self Compassion, and have begun teaching it. Learning to be open and allowing in the present moment has helped heal the worrying and overthinking. Sure, there is damage from the past, but there is a lot of wellness too.

Mindfulness has helped me to see the grace that is here in this moment where life is. It has helped me to focus on dealing with life as it unfolds. Life is more manageable and satisfying this way. I would love to be able to continue to share this practice with others.

Our thoughts, feelings, dreams - even our beliefs are felt through the body. They can be accessed and influenced by touch. A client came to me recently. She felt like she was coming down with an illness, but she had no pain or injuries at the moment to work on. I assured her we can always benefit from touch. I asked her how she'd like to feel. "Fearless and integrated!" she immediately said.

She lay down on my table, and I asked her to talk to me about fear. That morning a friend in her women's group was diagnosed with a terrible cancer. "I remembered another friend who had died two years ago of cancer."

"How did you feel then?" I asked.

"Hopeless." She had been with her friend and helped her as the cancer progressed. "My friend had no particular spiritual belief. But she was brave and she stayed so positive throughout. She was inspiring!"

My client wanted to be supportive of her current friend who needed support and was reaching out for spiritual protection. "What do you believe?" I asked her.

"I don't know."

I laid my hands on her shoulders and felt her breathing. I could feel the tightness that continued down through her chest. We went through all of the body. I would feel and reflect tension patterns.

Her body responded and made changes and relaxed. As the session came to an end, her body felt peaceful and she said she felt connected with an easy flow of energy. She no longer felt as if she was getting sick. At the end, she sat up and smiled. "I still don't know how I feel, but I am open to possibilities!" She was radiant!

When I think about my own healing, there is so much I do not understand. Sometimes it seems miraculous. Also when I work with others, there is much I can't explain.

Sometimes, I think I know what is going on with a person and what they need. When I put my hands on them, their body may tell me a different story. Their inner body usually has a clear sense of what it needs and what it can tolerate. I am always amazed.

I may feel a tension pattern and reflect it to the body so that the body will make the best change it can. I need only listen and follow the changes with my hands. When the body spontaneously heals an area, there is an atmosphere, an energy that is beautiful and feels effortless and reverent. When it blossoms with some quiet attention, it seems beyond their pain or anxiety or expectations. It seems eternal.

Mindfulness and meditation are important parts of my life. They are gateways, though. They lead me to another level of connection, someplace deep within yet encompassing everything. I feel in communion with a power much larger than myself.

My personal struggles and agendas fall away there. I lose that narrow sense of self, and find that in my expanded awareness there is a definite place for me. There I am completely accepted just as I am.

This is a place I would get to as a child with prayer. My prayers are different now - they are attempts to be open to the larger community - to be accepting and thankful. I feel I am walking with spirit there. This level is elusive as we go about our days, yet it is always there at the edges of our consciousness.

Picture a breath that we take in as we inhale. It is separated from the full field of air as we take it into our lungs. For that moment, it is ours. When we exhale, it is released out into the whole field once again, but this breath carries with it the signature of our having embodied it.

Some say that in this life we carry this spirit within us like a separate drop of water. And when we leave our body behind in death, that drop becomes once more a seamless part of the ocean of humanity. We arise from this entity and we return to it. This gives me a sense of peace and feels right and is one small place I can get to with my limited knowing.

I feel very blessed to have had many precious moments with my family and with my friends. I am cheered to have a glimpse into the future through the eyes of my amazing grandchildren: Juliet, Jayden, Noah and James. I have been fortunate to see many beautiful places.

I have been able to work with many lovely people over the years and to have seen them make many positive changes. The thought of not working makes me wonder if the days will feel as vital and if the light on those days will shine quite as brightly. I do need to wind down, though. That is part of the circle of life.

Like the pattern I would trace with my eyes along the borders of a ceiling during a therapy session, the circle brings you back to the same place in a new way. Looking closer, noticing the little encounters in each day, I see that we can in small ways always be of help to others. Working less would mean there would be less money for travel and nonessentials, but I look forward to life being a little simpler.

Of course I worry that my memory will be worse, but I've learned that memory doesn't truly make up who we are as individuals. We all lose ground with aging. So be it.

The one thing that has kept me going through tough times is the curiosity to see what is next. Despite everything, life and individuals have continued to surprise and delight me in new ways each day, and I am simply grateful.

In Time To Heal

I cannot believe
After all this time
There is still so much to heal.
So much from early years -
Years spent building
Strong arms and legs,
To bear time's battery.
Still so much to soothe
To understand
To tell ourselves :
"We matter, we are
Valued and brave,"
Words we hear now
Almost for the first time.
Will that small voice
Ever feel heard?
Will the little one inside
Ever completely blossom
Before the ages dry it
From the inside out,
And it wafts away?
Memories of healing
Form warm imprints
On that chilly wind.

Mary Alice Cullinan ~ August 2017

Poetry is A Bridge

Animated Cat

Who is this stalking my lumpy quilt?
Who poises to pounce on my covered foot?
Not now, Cato!
Who sighs when no one will dangle a string,
Or cries to the heavens for a fishy treat?
Who, fulfilled, slips off?
Who is this creature languidly licking each limb,
A foot high in yoga pose, she skims,
Every crevice clean.
She bids you scratch her head, and down, showing
Her silken tummy, a humming bird purring
Until claw draws the line.
I cradle her little head in my palm, such life!
I know her thoughts don't run as mine -
She's animation in present time.

Mary Alice Cullinan ~ August 2011

Healing

Healing is a lotus bud.
Seen from my window
In minted growing light
On a curling black stem
Near a full flower afire.
The roots of the bud
Moored deep into mud
Divine the way up.
A crease on pond's serene face,
Makes this a magical place.
Change floats like a low wave,
Lemon ebbs green, to soft pink.
Water flows into sky.
Tender soul in violet mist,
Mist of my soul,
Emerges clean as a dream.
A dream of unity,
The bud reaches out,
Meeting sun at horizon.
Balancing on point.
From the golden frame
I follow bud's journey,
My own heart unfolds.
In its own time,
A bloom.

Mary Alice Cullinan

Scars

When I was in my thirties
My mother had cancer.
She was uncomfortable
Was secret about it then.
One day I visited her in Florida.
She was beside me on the couch
She asked me if I would like
To see her scar.
It would be true then.
I knew she'd had a mastectomy
But it was dark and hidden
And we didn't talk about it.
I was curious and afraid.
Afraid I might shudder,
I might be overwhelmed, panic.
She unbuttoned her blouse
And there she wore a child's undershirt.
She pulled this up
And I saw the rugged, rough,
Red river of a line that swelled
And curled across her breastplate.
It was true in that moment
Her two columns that had been
Apart of her, a part of me and
My siblings' life, the white cups
That I had seen when she was sick,
That I'd notice had sagged a bit
With age, the nipples small and pink.

Those two staunch structures were felled
With one blade's swoop and
All that was left was a mass of scar tissue
And unhealed memories.
She rubbed her hand across the flat
And smiled and said "It's great,
I can sleep on my stomach now."

People come to New York to see
To see the place where once
Stood two towers, controversial,
But had become a part of the city.
They come out of curiosity,
Or fear that some could be so powerful
And angry and active.
They don't want it to be true
But come and stand and look
And see the ragged scar, Ground Zero.
And it becomes true and there is
Nothing to see but much to heal.
My mother didn't have reconstructive
Surgery, no cosmetics, no more.
She rubbed her hand across her chest
And smiled and let me see
Her fingers seeming to work the
Way to heal what lay beneath.

Mary Alice Cullinan

I See My Mother

I see my mother sick
Lying in her narrow wood bed,
Her covers lumped in a mound.

I am just a child
Looking into my brother's eyes.
We do not know what to do.

The house is falling down.
The trees in the yard are dying.
There is garbage in the street.

I stand beside her bed,
Twisting my hands, empty and stiff.
Why am I always the child?

I could brush her thin hair.
I could touch my brother's small face.
I could water the trees' roots.

I am 15 and dream,
I see myself wringing my hands,
Waiting for her to get up.

Wait, is someone coming?
My brother looks into *my* eyes
As if the answer's there.

Mary Alice Cullinan ~ May 1966

Forgive you, Father

If I forgive you, father,
I have to forgive the whole human race.
All this time I have clenched my bowels.
I have kept the tremors still.
I have set my insides in concrete
Against mere judgment from you.
Now they tell me it doesn't matter who you are.
Now they say we are many people all the time.
And I thought there was only one of me
Who wasn't good enough.
Do I pray my sparkle isn't just
A reflection of someone else's light
Waiting for approval?
Waiting always in the shadows for a father's nod.
If I can forgive me,
I can forgive a race of us.
If I can forgive everyone,
I can easily forgive you, father.
My belly rolls with laughter
As I release those lead balloons to the sky.
I wasn't quite as fragile as you thought.

Mary Alice Cullinan ~ June 1979

A Handmade Box

I poise at the edge of me to hold you.
A wave bends back, its crest -
A clear blue line -
The horizon separating sea from sky,
Sorting the wash of urgency
Into the calm cloth of health.

I stay dearly with that line,
Cradling your essence, your mind's bones.
My hands bear the weight of your life.
Curving your foot, I am moved by your wonder.
My border nears your border and bows.
Spirit arrives trembling on the brink of hush.

Together we create a box, a box
Whose sides are made of trust
A secure container to be sure,
A coffer of possibilities, a field
Where we work and discard "try"
As the music of awe plays on.

I lift your heel, this box is enough
To support and allow the light passage,
A foot links ankle and hip, expanding box.
Adding shoulder, I anchor, you guide me.
Your body packs this case for a short trip.
I sink to ocean's floor, for the long haul.

My right hand draws your head to me,
At your neck, a mermaid combs seaweed.
Box slides through box, ships in the night,
Separate paths in the wake of stardust.
We balance the light of suns
To the density of our bones.

Behind my eyes, I sense untangling, the eddies
That toss us, have set us down in stiller waters.
The box fades, leaving in its wake
Blue lines to line heart's chambers.
We quiver at such limitlessness,
We dance on. The box we make is love.

Mary Alice Cullinan ~ October 2017

Today is A Good Day to Die

I told my plants that today was a good day to die.
It is cold on the porch except for some sun. I haul them.
Each night I bring them into the hot kitchen
with radiators and cooking smells.
Each morning I set them out on a layer of frost
grown wide on the stones.
It isn't much of a life for them,
not like the summer days of grand light.
The summer nights of mist and moon
and music on the breezes.
Then the change of weather is welcome,
a surprise, not a threat, enchanted.
But now, now it's just a waiting game,
stolen breaths, stagnant time.

Mary Alice Cullinan ~ October 1991

On The First Day of Summer

I woke up this first
Morning of summer and
Waited a long moment
Before I put my feet to the floor.
Brief dreams were brushed aside
With the dusting swirls of the sun.
Purrs stirred from my belly to my chest
In light's dancing shapeless shifts.
The day's small plans slipped sideways
At the revving of the engine within.
The mind-deafening hum
Cleared the way for change.
Oh, to be in my room without wallpaper
On this day of all days –
The longest day of the year.
The one you show up to
Is that long, luscious day.

Mary Alice Cullinan ~ June 21, 2008

All of Us

All of us
Wish to rise
To the surface of our lives,
Creating something priceless.
Our life may be the masterpiece.
Our drives slash broad strokes across the wash -
Rushing to the front lines of battle,
Helping a woman in an alley give birth,
Making cupcakes for the PTA at midnight.
The strands within us are the mix,
We dip the brush and lift.

All of us wish to rise
To the water's top.
Some are hooked, dragged down
By heart disease, dyslexia, depression.
These jagged, broken stones
Lurking in the coal black depths.
Cannot we step upon them,
Ever upwards in our thirst?
Water lilies unfold as art
To the forever sun above.

Mary Alice Cullinan ~ April 1985

Slipping Into the Sea of Yin

I don't know how to swim
In the soft sea of yin
(To swim and not to drown).

I don't know how to float
When tides flow slowly in
(Allowing, sinking down).

I do not feel afraid
Of the Sea Dragon's tongue
(Though swallowed, I may ache).

I flee the sucking whorls
Smothering hopes for morn
(And I'm lost in awake).

I don't know how to court
Dreams that float with ease
(Reach out and not to fight).

I'm not a fish or eel
Slipping through waves of peace
(I just can't sleep at night).

Mary Alice Cullinan ~ June 2003

75

Fifty

I am fifty
And full of dust
Furnace of ashes
By products of lust.
As my soft core
Draws in to dry
My skin's a bath,
I long to cry.
I am brimming
With love and regret
I dare not stem
A rising torrent.
A sun is west
Red streams glisten,
Who will allow.
Who will listen?
My woman chums
talk teas and herbs
And soy and creams
and thinning pubes.
But who will sit
Across from me
And take my hand
And let me grieve?
I can't unfold
A homemade child,
From this womb,
All seed's exiled.
And so my heart

Scorns middle spread.
I've no need to
Turn a man's head.
When asked what makes
Me womanly?
Hard cold facts of
Biology.
How sad you can't
They may soothe,
Surely you don't
want to, do you?
The change is come,
I bravely come,
Do I trade sex
For wan wisdom?
Ironic smile,
I dry my eyes,
I have no choice,
I will be wise.
Creation has no
Pain to embrace,
Weathered choices
Etched on my face.
In separate beds
These rivers flow,
Sailing past bridges
By undertow.

Mary Alice Cullinan

Goodness Grows

There is no good seed. There is only seed.
Dropped to earth is a perfectly potent bomb.
All of its flaws intact.
Jagged barbs beneath flawless baby skin.
Don't worry, take my hand
I want to show you
My favorite place in the woods.
Mind the path, it is difficult to find,
Overgrown in summer's sudden intensity,
This trail is little used.
Here there are masses of brambles
Seek deep in for the sweet meat,
though it's mostly picked clean.
I love the berries' perfectly sweet, just-ripe taste.
The trick is to step on their grasping runners ,
Running close to the ground
Or they will tear your legs to shreds.
The bushes exploded after a dry spell this year.
Relentless spring showers bombarded, too many.
Though we all love all kinds of showers – even baby….

Mary Alice Cullinan ~ July 2010

Winter's Flight

One wintry night
Wind spewing frozen rain
A hammering upon my door,
Shattering stillness came.
Heart racing, I cringed, hung back
Who would would shake this home
With heartless shattering blasts?
I who never turned a soul away,
Inviting one and all within
Not minding my own stirring
But to theirs I tried to hasten.
I am no saint but fearing
That a selfish being
Stands alone and wretched in the
Final measuring.
Shivering I undid the latch
Wishing now to be free
A dying bird was nailed there,
Broken, trapped and sadly me.

Mary Alice Cullinan ~ February 2016

Do Not Dry Clean

You magically appear, my kitty,
To pounce upon the running shorts
Laid out across the bed.
I wrestle with wrinkled pajamas,
As you dive on the cotton sweats,
Sliding a paw into a cloth leg.
You are vexed by the enormous cuff,
And roll the lot into a ball.
These sad clothes are not for you
You - always dressed to the nines in a tux -
Looking elegant and well-pressed
Despite the hours sunbathing.
Do not envy me my manufactured threads.
If I had a coat like you, black and white
Relief in such soft, luxurious fur,
I should be oh so happy and relaxed.
You glide in your perfectly fitted dress,
Warm in winter and surprisingly cool
In humidity and heat.
I should never worry of what to wear and
Wonder if it's right for the occasion.
I'd know it did not go against fair trade
And no animals were harmed in its making.
Oh, to have what you take for granted
I'd be the queen of prêt-á-porter.
My outfit would stay in peak condition, I suppose,
As long as I licked myself up and down
Throughout the day.
Are you sure you can't be dry cleaned?

Mary Alice Cullinan ~ June 2014

Snow Passage

I waited all day for the snow
To change over to rain.
In the silvery morning light.
Dynamic clouds had rolled across a blue sky.
Each snowflake a gift.
By lunchtime, great piles gathered in tree crotches.
Finger-like branches
Coated themselves with marshmallow stickiness.
Despite the forecasts,
It kept coming down.
In late afternoon,
Weary pearls were no longer precious ,
Adding their weight to the grey fogginess -
A middle-aged spread.
Night quietly fell along with the snow.
I withdrew to flannel and down.
In the middle of the night,
I awoke to the bracing upbeat of rain
Dancing on the roof,
On the road,
On the woods,
Diving into snowdrifts outside my bedroom window.
I could see finally the bare, leafless tree limbs,
Shimmering black and clean in the icy wet.
Stark sentinels against its blanket of peaceful snow.

Mary Alice Cullinan

Yoga on Rosh Hashanah

Tonight begins Rosh Hashanah
A new year
A new moon
A Time of beginning.
This morning we do yoga together.
It is sunny and the air is crisp.
People are smiling
We struggle to open our hearts
Even in the most difficult poses.
Suspended shakily between one bended knee
And one long leg thrust back,
Rooting into Mother Earth,
We work to pull our legs
Toward each other,
Creating a firmer, clearer, stronger base.
Searching deeply within to find balance
With all about us,
We tentatively raise our torso,
Climbing higher and steadier
With each breath until we are able to
Triumphantly lift our arms high overhead
To let our hearts swell toward heaven.
The wash of graceful ascent and ability
Lifts us even higher and fills our being with joy.
And at just that moment -
When it is almost too much joy to bear -
We offer what we have created to
Something much bigger than ourselves.

Our practice and our posture becomes one
Not of attainment but of supplication and gratitude.
Not needing to sustain the weight of such beauty,
We can relax and be
Like a wave softening and sinking
To rejoin and become part of the larger ocean
Once more.
Seamless with the surface this great body,
We are drops of water connected even to the darkest depth.
In the giving up the struggle and the holding on,
We are born again
A new beginning with each breath,
Each new moon,
Each Rosh Hashanah.
Able to bask in the mystery and beauty of life and yoga.

Mary Alice Cullinan ~ September 24, 2014

When I Am Aware

When I am aware
Rested, still,
It kicks in.
The whole world
Expands then shrinks
To a point and I
Am the smallest part
Of that point and
Open.

I am sorry -
So sorry for being,
Being somewhere else,
Asleep, selfish.
It doesn't matter what.
The sadness is the gateway.
Aching and tearful
I am blessedly alive.

A channel opens to
Infinite presence
With my prayer.
Who says prayers are
Never answered?

The connection would
Be enough, but from
The void begins a
Tickling, ripple of
Laughter floating.

Don't sweat the small stuff -
The roots of absurdity.
Then the rush, lifting beyond
River beds and rocks
And clouds -
Hilarious, blinding light.

Mary Alice Cullinan ~ June 9, 2017

The Squeeze Box

Here I am
Trying to be cool
And then
The words slip out
And everything stops.
All eyes around turn
A harsh light on me.
"That was not cool."
"You are not cool."

A hand forms a fist in my gut
With a wire at its center,
Pulled down down down
To the bottom of my belly.
My cheeks burn bright and hot.
This is not helping me to disappear.
My heart hurts as if poked
With a lit sparkler.

Before I can inhale,
My insides crush together.
Will it ever stop?
I don't know. I wonder
As I let it be as painful as it needs to be
In this moment.

I unclench my fist
Cradling the wired contraption which
In my hands has become
An accordion that was squeezed shut.

And now this box begins to breathe -
In and out and
In and out -
Making music -
Funky music to be sure.
And the words slipped out
20 years ago.
But now they are merely
Lyrics to an old song.

Mary Alice Cullinan ~ June 1, 2016

Only Breath

There is nothing to fix
I am broken
There is nothing to fix
Waves wash over me

Crashing in glass shards on the shore.
Salty tears are sucked through sand
Returning to the churning pump

The heart of my belly
Leaning against my spine
Begins to beat
Fueled by the fire pit heating up
At my navel.

The dome of this heart swells
to inflate the dome of my diaphragm
And breath is the alchemist.
Dry transforms into a water troll.

Grief wells up and and flows.
The umbrella of my lungs
Expands the dome of my
Beating heart -
Sadness spilling up and out

"Why didn't my mother protect me
from all the sadness in the world?"
My inner child wails.

And the surf simply breaks.
"Why couldn't I protect my children
From the sadness in the world?"
And my face aches and shatters.

"Why can't I protect me from
The sadness in the world?"
And I think maybe it's one true
Thing I can do.....

There is nothing to fix
I am whole
There is nothing to fix
There is only breath.

Mary Alice Cullinan

Creative Memories

An artist at the co-op
Showed me his photos -
Stunning scenes,
Collages of sky and water
And trees
From different places
And different times fused
In one coherent vision.
A fisherman under a Cape May pier,
A sunset from Key West,
A maple whose leaves are
Changing from green to orange
To the color of a cloud in the Chesapeake.
A lone heron stands
Against a peeling beige fence,
Traces of pink mute the cottony sky.
The bare trees reflected upside down
In a still, grey pond -
All capture a sense of loneliness
Or is it solitude?
Is it "fake" art to cut and paste
These stored images,
Creating something that never really was?
But isn't this just like our memory?
A bird from a beach walk,
A fence from our childhood home,
The pond of a lost teen summer,
The grey before a sunrise,
The pink of a toy animal held tight,

All selected in an instant,
Assembled as we try to reconnect with
Another time, another place,
Another us on our way to the "true" here
And now,
Fleeting as that is.

Mary Alice Cullinan ~ September 2017

All Your Life You Spend

All your life you spend judging.
One day you wake up and realize
There is nothing to judge.
A life's work erased with one keystroke.
What a relief!

Mary Alice Cullinan

A Journey

A journey is born
Out of a confusion
Of place.

Stretching out a foot,
Testing the earth
With a toe

You reach for a star.
A poem is the bridge
That carries you there.

Your fingers read
The raised text of
A foreign tongue.

You alight on a word -
The word lights the gray
Glass of your eyes.

Is the thought newborn?
Or a filtered dust speck from
One long forgotten?

Ears decipher heart's code,
The sign language of ghosts,
The weight of a circle.

A phrase guides your hand
Up the rungs of a ladder
Out of ground's safety.

Is this trip to a better perch?
For a moment, you can see
Your house from the sky.

September 14, 2017 Mary Alice Cullinan

I Am A Prayer Flag

I am a prayer flag
Rippling in the breeze.
At times I feel I'm made
Of strings so light
The slightest wind
Skimming the lip of a pond
Would shake my inners
To all four corners.
I fly, and furl and unfurl
And each time I quake,
A prayer is made to all.
In cold, stiff downpours
I flap and flutter on
To bend the universe's ear.
I know my prayers are heard
The sun comes out anew
And I unfold totally whole.
The wrinkles in my fabric
Write for all to read,
A story of survival.

Mary Alice Cullinan ~ January 2013

Made in the USA
Middletown, DE
10 November 2017